DISCARDED

from

New Hanover County Public Library

W9-BYX-881

First Facts

Community Helpers at Work

A Day in the
Life of a
Teacher

by Heather Adamson

Consultant:
Dr. Adele Greenlee
Professor of Education
Bethel College
St. Paul, Minnesota

Capstone
press

Mankato, Minnesota

NEW HANOVER COUNTY
PUBLIC LIBRARY
201 CHESTNUT STREET
WILMINGTON, NC 28401

First Facts is published by Capstone Press
151 Good Counsel Drive, P.O. Box 669, Mankato, Minnesota 56002
http://www.capstone-press.com

Copyright © 2004 by Capstone Press. All rights reserved.
No part of this publication may be reproduced in whole or in part, or stored in a retrieval system, or transmitted in any form or by any means, electronic, mechanical, photocopying, recording, or otherwise, without written permission of the publisher.
For information regarding permission, write to Capstone Press,
151 Good Counsel Drive, P.O. Box 669, Dept. R, Mankato, Minnesota 56002.
Printed in the United States of America

Library of Congress Cataloging-in-Publication Data
Adamson, Heather, 1974–
  A day in the life of a teacher / by Heather Adamson.
    p. cm.—(First facts. Community helpers at work)
  Includes bibliographical references and index
  Contents: How do teachers start their days?—Do teachers work alone?—How do teachers know what to teach each day?—Where do teachers eat lunch?—What do teachers read?—What do teachers do while students are at other classes?—What do teachers do after school?—Do teachers have homework?—Diagram.
    ISBN 0-7368-2286-0 (hardcover)
  1. Elementary school teachers—Juvenile literature. 2. Elementary school teaching—Vocational guidance—Juvenile literature. [1. Teachers. 2. Occupations.]
I. Title. II. Series.
LB1776.A33 2004
372.11—dc21   2003000781

Credits
Jennifer Schonborn, designer; Jim Foell, photographer; Eric Kudalis, product planning editor

Photo Credits
All photos by Capstone Press/Jim Foell except page 20 (left) from the State Historical Society of Iowa.

Artistic Effects
Capstone Press, Ingram Publishing, PhotoDisc

Special thanks to Mary Chan and everyone at Northport Elementary School of Brooklyn Center, Minnesota, for their help in photographing this book.

1 2 3 4 5 6 08 07 06 05 04 03

Table of Contents

How do teachers start their days?

Teachers go to school early. They get ready to teach. Mrs. Chan gathers the things her second graders will use today. She finds colored paper and makes copies of a math worksheet. She writes the reading groups on the board. She sorts corrected papers into folders.

Fun Fact:
Most schools in the United States meet 180 days each year. Schools in some countries meet for 240 days each year.

7:00 in the morning

Do teachers work alone?

It takes teamwork to run a school. Before the students arrive, some of the school's staff meet. They plan the science fair. After the meeting, Mrs. Chan picks up today's announcements. The secretary tells Mrs. Chan a new student will be joining her class.

7:30 in the morning

How do teachers know what to teach each day?

Teachers use guides to plan lessons for each day. The guides tell teachers what each grade must learn. Fractions are part of the second-grade guide. Today, Mrs. Chan uses paper pizzas to explain fractions to the class.

9:30 in the morning

9

11:00 in the morning

Where do teachers eat lunch?

Teachers usually eat lunch with other school workers. Mrs. Chan eats her lunch in the staff room. She tells Mr. Green about a movie she saw. They talk about a field trip idea for the second and third grades.

Fun Fact:

The tradition of bringing apples to teachers may be related to fall. The school year always began after the fall harvest when apples were ripe.

11

12:30 in the
afternoon

12

What do teachers read?

Reading is important to teachers. During recess, Mrs. Chan reads lesson ideas. After recess, she reads a book to her class. Then, she helps students write their own stories. She will read them later.

What do teachers do while students are at other classes?

Teachers always stay busy. While her students are at music class, Mrs. Chan uses a computer. She types out next week's spelling words. Mrs. Chan also sets up a conference to meet with a student's parents.

Fun Fact:

The first chalkboard was used in a school in Philadelphia in 1809.

15

1:00 in the
afternoon

What do teachers do after school?

Teachers have work to do after school. Mrs. Chan helps students pick books for the reading club. Then, she puts up a new bulletin board. She stores the old one to use next year.

3:00 in the afternoon

Do teachers have homework?

Teachers often take work home. Mrs. Chan packs her briefcase with folders of papers. She will correct the papers after she eats supper with her family. She will also make a list of items she needs for tomorrow's lessons. Teaching is hard work. But Mrs. Chan loves to see her students learning each day!

5:00 in the
evening

19

Map

Computer

Textbooks

Amazing But True!

In the 1800s, most teachers worked in one-room schoolhouses. Stoves heated the schools. Teachers chopped the wood for the stoves. Sometimes teachers gave this chore to misbehaving students.

Glossary

announcement (uh-NOUNSS-ment)—official information that needs to be said out loud; teachers make announcements to their students about lunch menus and events.

briefcase (BREEF-kayss)—a bag with a handle, used for carrying papers

bulletin board (BUL-uht-tuhn BORD)—a decorated area on the wall where information is presented

conference (KON-fur-uhnss)—a meeting to discuss ideas and opinions; teachers have conferences with parents to tell them how their children are doing in class.

staff (STAFF)—a group of people who work for the same company or organization

Read More

Hallinan, P. K. *My Teacher's My Friend.* Nashville: Ideals Children's Books, 2001.

Hayward, Linda. *A Day in the Life of a Teacher.* Dorling Kindersley Readers. New York: DK, 2001.

Vogel, Elizabeth. *Meet My Teacher.* My School. New York: PowerKids Press, 2002.

Internet Sites

Do you want to find out more about teachers? Let FactHound, our fact-finding hound dog, do the research for you.

Here's how:

1) Visit *http://www.facthound.com*

2) Type in the **Book ID** number: **0736822860**

3) Click on **FETCH IT**.

FactHound will fetch Internet sites picked by our editors just for you!

Index

04/04

Growing Readers
New Hanover County Public Library
201 Chestnut Street
Wilmington, NC 28401